STOP.
AF604599
YAY!

WAIT,

SAYS THE COMMA

BY ROB LISLE

First Published 2026 by
Redback Publishing
Suite 6, 13a Narabang Way,
Belrose NSW 2085
Australia

www.redbackpublishing.com
orders@redbackpublishing.com

ISBN 978-1-761402-14-2

Author: Rob Lisle
Editor: Simone Saba
Designer: Redback Publishing
Illustrator: Rob Lisle

Originated by Redback Publishing

A catalogue record for this book is available from the National Library of Australia

WAIT,

SAYS THE COMMA

If you run out of breath reading a sentence, you might need a comma.
Look at those birds having fun, so free, flying high with nothing in their way, able to go wherever they want.
I'm going to fly, because if they can do it, so can I.
Nothing beats fetching a ball, or a good belly rub, but smelling your mate's butt is the best.

Dug, you're a dog, and dogs don't fly. We eat, run, sleep and poop ... that's it.
And it's such a perfect life, I bet those birds probably wish they were dogs.
Chilling in the pool, taking random naps, receiving endless love and pats, taking a run with the wind in your fur, they all make being a dog awesome.
But, Dug still wants more.

Use a comma after an **introductory word** or **phrase**.

Whiskers, you can't bother me up here.
Silly pooch, the swing will bring you right back to me.
Hey Pete, I can see your house from here.
Oh yeah, looks kinda small.

Use commas to add **extra information** into a sentence.

The sky looks beautiful, so blue, from this angle.
I would catch you, Big Billy, but you look really heavy.
Careful not to hit your head, or the rest of you, on the ground.
Flying Attempt, number 367, 1 June 2055.

Use commas between two **descriptive** words.

You look like you could use a cool, feathered, funky hat.
I actually have one on my long, spotty tail.
HATS, HATS, HATS.
ROCKET LAUNCH TONIGHT
ES, COSTUMES.

Use commas to separate items in a **list**.

POST COMPLAINTS TO: 321 Fake Street, Nowhere, 1234

When writing a full address in a sentence,
use commas to separate the different parts of the location.

Use a comma when calling someone by **name**.

Dad, I want the red dragon kite.
Mikey, that's a lobster.
Terry, that looks like the one for us.
I think you're right, Tony.

Use a comma before joining words like **and, but, or,** and **so,** if they link two full sentences.

You need an extra boost, like a rocket, but where would you get one?
I have a good idea, or at least I *think* I do.

Use commas to set off **short expressions** that show emotion.

$2
SOLD OUT
$5
SOLD OUT
$4
OUT
$2
$3
$4
$8
$3,000
Wowza, big audience tonight.
Aww, I want to see it launch.
Oh no, I'm going down.
Err, what's this for?

Use commas in sentences with little **questions** at the end.

Dogs can't fly, can they?
He touched both wires, didn't he?
Frank, you're okay, right?
This should be entertaining, don't you think?

Use commas when saying something **again** and **again**.

That dog looks very, very sore.
Let's go faster, faster, faster!
Look at our kite go up, up, up!

So many reasons it's important to **wait**.

Not so fast, take a breath and practise.

Now that you're a COMMA master, can you practise your new skills by describing what these characters are doing?

Can you describe these characters really clearly, with all the fun details, so someone else can draw them?

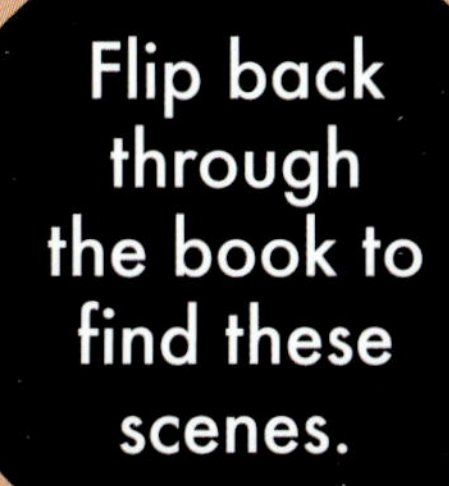
Flip back through the book to find these scenes.

$4

ACTIVITIES

COMMA SWITCHEROO

OBJECTIVE	Discover how comma placement changes meaning.	
STEPS	• Read two similar sentences to the children, one with commas and one without. • Talk about how the meaning or tone is different. • Ask the children to write 'before and after' sentences using a comma.	**EXAMPLES** Let's eat Dug! Let's eat, Dug!
BONUS ACTIVITY	Children can make a comic strip with both versions and fun drawings.	

COMA SCIENTIST

OBJECTIVE	Use commas to write instructions.	
STEPS	• Have students think of a made-up flying device (wings, rocket boots, chicken jet pack). • They must write a list of materials they will need to make their flying device. • Read all the inventions out loud or draw blueprints.	**EXAMPLE** Use old boots, flamethrowers, sticky tape and a helmet.
BONUS ACTIVITY	Create an 'Inventor's Handbook' to keep in the classroom.	

ADJECTIVE ARTIST

OBJECTIVE	Use commas between adjectives that describe something.
STEPS	• Have children select a character from the book. • Ask them to think of three words to describe it. • Have them write a sentence using those adjectives with commas between them.
BONUS ACTIVITY	Children can use their imagination to draw a made-up creature and label it with three describing words.

EXAMPLE

The white, small, cheeky bird pooped in the fountain.

DETAIL DETECTIVES

OBJECTIVE	Practise using commas to add extra details around a noun.
STEPS	• Tell kids to select an animal or object from this book and write a simple statement about where it is or what it is doing. • Tell them to think of one or two fun details about it (like what colour it is, or what kind of personality does it have). • Have them write a new sentence with the extra information, adding commas around the descriptions.
BONUS ACTIVITY	Have the children write two sentences, one without extra info and one with. They can then compare what picture comes to their mind when they read each sentence.

EXAMPLE

Leo sells kites.

Leo, the friendly lion, sells kites.

NARRATIVE TEXT

In his quest to learn how to fly, Dug went to visit the local costume store. On display he saw all sorts of outfits like a Viking helmet, a superhero suit, a bunny outfit, a mouse mask and many different hats.

He asked the storekeeper, a tall giraffe, if there was anything in the store that could help him fly.

"These large, pink wings will do the trick." The storekeeper handed Dug the wings, which came with a cool bird hat.

Dug put them on his back, ready for his next attempt at flying.

COMMA TREASURE HUNT

OBJECTIVE	Identify and understand commas in real text.	
STEPS	• Have the kids copy out the provided narrative, ensuring they include every comma. • Have them circle or highlight every comma found. • Discuss what kind of comma it is (list, pause, adjective).	**EXAMPLES** *These large, pink wings will do the trick.* The comma separates two descriptive words.
BONUS ACTIVITY	Hide comma cards around the classroom and have the children search for them. They must read the card out loud when they find it.	

COMMA PAUSE PATROL

OBJECTIVE	Recognise how commas make a pause in a sentence.
STEPS	• Read the provided narrative out loud. • Read each sentence twice: - First, read it without pausing at the commas. - Then, read it again with a little pause at each comma. • Tell the children to listen for the difference. Ask them which one sounds better or clearer? • Ask them to now try writing their own funny or dramatic sentence. • Remind them to add commas where they want the reader to pause!
BONUS ACTIVITY	Children can create a 'Pause or Panic' poster showing how commas save the day.

EXAMPLES

No dogs allowed.
No, dogs allowed.

COMMA PARADE

OBJECTIVE	Use commas in a list of action words.
STEPS	• Choose a spread from this book. • Have the kids act out or name the actions on the page. • Kids can then write a sentence listing the actions, using commas.
BONUS ACTIVITY	Build one big class sentence and act it out!

EXAMPLE

The dogs on the trampoline jumped, bounced, flipped and fell.

COLLECT ALL THE BOOKS IN THE PUNCTUATION EXPEDITION SERIES!
Dad, there's more fun-packed, brain-boosting books to get.
PUNCTUATION EXPEDITION
HUH? ASKS THE QUESTION MARK
How?
Who?
Where?
What?
Why?
ROB LISLE
PUNCTUATION EXPEDITION
STOP. COMMANDS THE FULL STOP
Stop.
Woof.
Halt.
ROB LISLE
PUNCTUATION EXPEDITION
WAIT, SAYS THE COMMA
Wait,
Breathe,
Pause,
ROB LISLE
PUNCTUATION EXPEDITION
YAY! SHOUTS THE EXCLAMATION MARK
Yay!
Wow!
Woo!
Yeah!
Oink!
ROB LISLE

WAIT,
HUH?